A MODERN METHOD FOR PIANO SCALES

Suzanna Sifter

This book is dedicated in memory of my mother,
Magdalene Liptay.

Cover photo courtesy of Steinway & Sons

BERKLEE PRESS

Editor in Chief: Jonathan Feist
Senior Vice President of Online Learning and Continuing Education/CEO of Berklee Online: Debbie Cavalier
Vice President of Enrollment Marketing and Management: Mike King
Vice President of Academic Strategy: Carin Nuernberg
Editorial Assistant: Brittany McCorriston

ISBN 978-0-87639-222-5

Berklee
Press

1140 Boylston Street • MS-855BP
Boston, MA 02215-3693 USA

Visit Berklee Press Online at
www.berkleepress.com

Berklee Online

Study music online at
online.berklee.edu

DISTRIBUTED BY

HAL•LEONARD®
7777 W. BLUEMOUND RD. P.O. BOX 13819
MILWAUKEE, WISCONSIN 53213

Visit Hal Leonard Online
www.halleonard.com

Berklee Press, a publishing activity of Berklee College of Music, is a not-for-profit educational publisher.
Available proceeds from the sales of our products are contributed to the scholarship funds of the college.

CONTENTS

ACKNOWLEDGMENTS

I would like to thank Piano Department Chair Dave Limina for his support in this project, Jonathan Feist for his excellent ideas and feedback, my amazing colleagues at Berklee for our great discussions relating to scales and modes, my students for teaching me how to teach, and most of all, my dear friends for their unwavering friendship and encouragement.

INTRODUCTION

Why study scales? Let's think about this. Clearly, we will not be performing technical scales on stage! The study of scales creates knowledge and ability well beyond technical skill. It is certainly essential for the improviser, and also paramount to the composer, songwriter, theorist, and performer, regardless of genre. Scales clearly spell major, minor, augmented, and diminished triads and seventh chords as well as tensions, which pave the way for interpreting lead sheets. Scales teach the fundamental fingerings that help navigate the topography of the keyboard.

The indispensable study of the major scale in all twelve keys sets the groundwork for learning to spell modes and the varied minor, pentatonic, blues, and symmetric scales. All in all, the study of scales is essential for every musician!

KEY SIGNATURES

There are various ways to notate the key signatures and fingerings for scales and modes. In this book, the major key signature is used for major parent scales, and the minor key signature is used for minor parent scales. Each chapter begins with the new scale's degree numberings, presented as they relate to the major scale.

FINGERINGS

Each finger is numbered: 1 = thumb, 2 = index finger, 3 = middle finger, 4 = ring finger, and 5 = "pinky" finger

Standard major scale fingering for the right hand begins with 1 on the root, and continues (1)23 1234. For the left hand, the standard fingering is 54321 321. Any other fingering is considered non-standard. The major-scale fingerings for C, G, D, E, and A all are standard. In F, the left hand is also standard, while the right hand breaks from the pattern due to the fact the fourth degree is a black key. So the fingering for F with the right hand is 1234 1234.

Scales that start on black keys use amended standard fingerings, often keeping the 123 1234 (right hand) but starting on a note *other than the tonic* (e.g., key of D♭, D♭ is the tonic). In the key of D♭, the right hand starts the pattern 123 on scale degree 7 (C), and continues with the thumb again on scale degree 3. The left-hand pattern 321 starts with 3 on the tonic and continues with finger 4 on G♭.

When working with flat keys, look for the white keys and determine where the thumb plays. Then you can see how the pattern plays out. Sometimes, the fingering of the parent scale is used in modal fingering. Remember the 4th finger rule: the

4th finger should only be played *once* within the octave. (This will become more apparent in modes.)

While most scales and modes avoid the use of the thumb on black keys, sometimes it is inescapable. Some pentatonic and blues scales also use 1313, or 123 12. This is also found in symmetric scales.

When working out a fingering, use this order:

1. Standard fingering
2. Non-standard/amended standard fingering
3. Fingering of parent scale
4. Combinations of 123, 13, or 12

Fingerings can be personalized depending on a pianist's particular hands and preferences. But we all have five fingers! I encourage you to implement the fingerings in this book, especially if you are new to playing scales—and particularly the symmetric and any unfamiliar modes. After studying these fingerings, you can make an educated decision on any alterations you may prefer.

TECHNIQUE

Fingers 2 and 3 are generally stronger than fingers 4 and 5. Working with scales can even out this deficiency. Take care to play the dynamic and sound the same between all fingers. Use minimal motion in your fingers when they are not being played. Keep your hand and wrist flexible, and use your arm to carry your hand up and down the keyboard.

NOTATION

In many of this book's exercises, you will notice stems going up and down for each note of the scales. For ease of reading, the fingerings on top are for the right hand, and the fingerings on the bottom are for the left hand. Play the scales an octave apart. When scales are notated only for one octave, the top note's fingering is labeled for continuing to the next octave. Depending on the scale, you may end with 5/1 (or other fingerings), then descend the keyboard. The goal is to play the scales for four octaves; however, one or two octaves are a good starting point.

MODES

Modes are a series of notes built from each degree of a given scale, called the parent scale. Modes of scales can be thought of in two ways: as the root being a scale degree of the parent scale, or the root being the root of a mode. Both ways are correct. For example, you can think of D Dorian as a C major scale starting on D, or a D Dorian starting on D. They are both the same notes, but the tonal center is different. It is recommended to play and hear the modes beginning on their roots—that is, D Dorian on D.

CHORD SCALES

The relationship of scales and their chords is very important—especially for the improviser and composer. The best way to think of this is to build a seventh chord from the root of any scale or mode. For instance, the major scale yields a Maj7 chord, and the Mixolydian mode yields a dominant 7 chord. So you can use the major scale to improvise/compose over a Maj7 chord, and the Mixolydian mode for a dominant 7 chord.

CREATING BACKING TRACKS

Many musicians work with a digital audio workstation (DAW) for recording and producing audio files. Some use GarageBand; others may have rhythms that are a part of their keyboards. Many of these tools provide drum loops that you can use to create drum tracks for practicing.

The directions for many songs and improvisation examples in this book recommend playing with a drum track. There are many reasons for this—the main reason being that it's fun! It will help you play with tempo accuracy and a good feel.

It is very important to practice the scales in this book in real musical settings, such as with vamps and backing tracks. You can also create bass lines to these tracks, add the suggested left-hand chords, and play melodies or improvise with your right hand. As you advance in your skills, you will be able to play live sessions! Backing tracks are a good start.

Tips:

- Set a tempo at which you are comfortable playing the example.

- Play in four- to eight-bar phrases.

- Make the track easy to play along with. Don't make it overly complex.

- Remember that the purpose of the track is to keep you in good time and aid your practice routine.

Listening lists at the end of each chapter suggest some music that is based on the different scale types, with some of my favorite performers. When you listen to any music, try to identify the scales being used.

As you begin your journey on learning new scales and modes, I wish you the excitement and joy of discovering new sounds to widen your intellectual and aural palette. Foremost, always use your ear, and enjoy!

Suzanna M. Sifter, 2022
Professor, Piano Department
Berklee College of Music

CHAPTER 1

The Mother Scale: Major

The major scale is a series of half steps and whole steps that form a seven-note linear formation.

The interval structure is: W W ½ W W W ½.

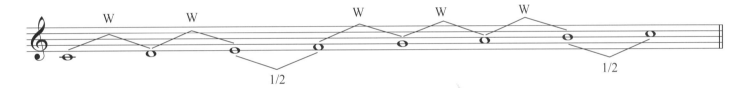

FIG. 1.1. C Major Scale Interval Structure

In studying scales and modes, it is of great importance to know, understand, and be able to play the major scale in twelve keys. The reason for this is that *all* other scales and modes can be compared to the major scale, with accidentals. For example, if the major scale is numbered 1 2 3 4 5 6 7, natural minor (also called Aeolian) is numbered 1 2 ♭3 4 5 ♭6 ♭7. This is a concise and uncomplicated way of learning scales and modes in any key because the numbers for a particular scale or mode will remain the same regardless of the key.

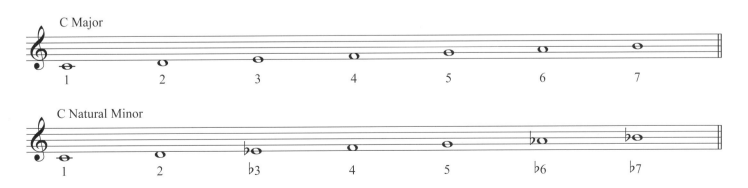

FIG. 1.2. C Major Scale vs. C Natural Minor (Aeolian) Scale

TWELVE KEY STUDY

Practice the major scale in all twelve keys with the correct fingerings, as labeled in figure 1.3.

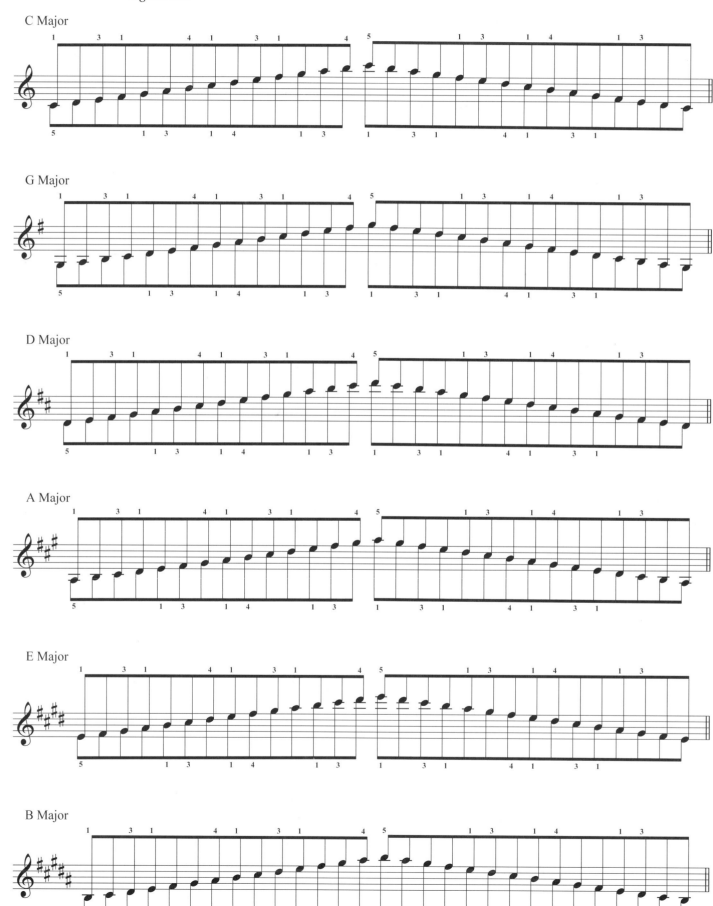

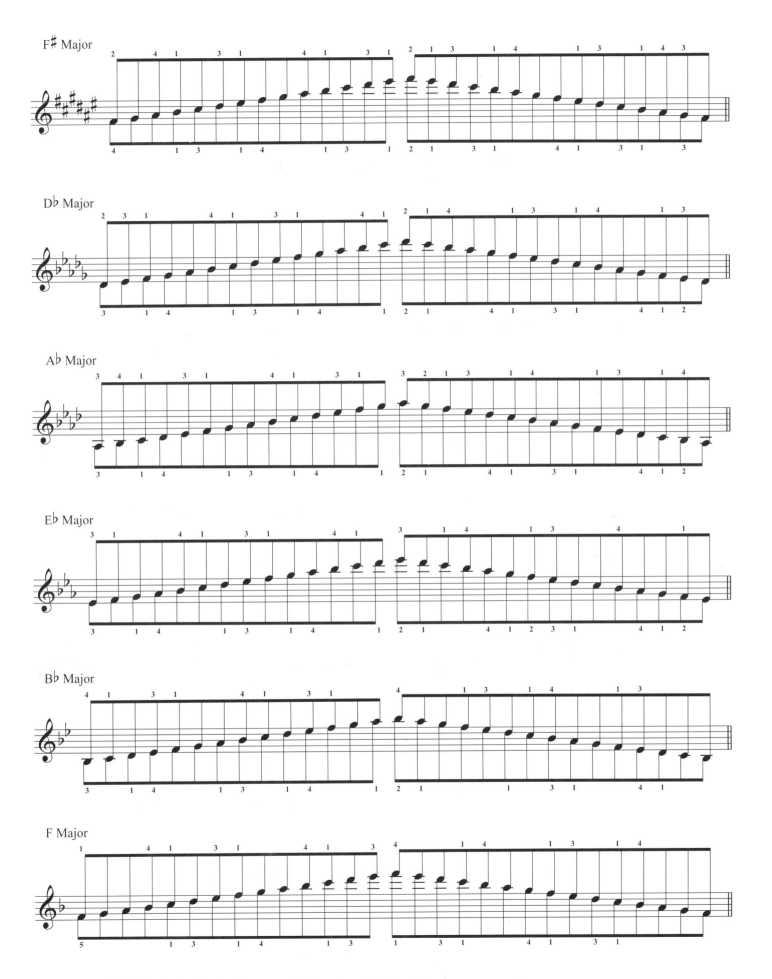

FIG. 1.3. Major Scale Notes and Fingerings in Two Octaves

Often when studying a scale or key for the first time, students can play each hand well separately but run into difficulty when putting the hands together. This is a common problem!

The solution to this is practice, practice, practice! Drill each hand many, many times, to the point that you not only get it right, but that *you can't get it wrong*. Then put your hands together slowly—even out of time, first.

Do not rush this method. When you introduce a new skill to your mind, ears, and hands, it is fertile ground. Mistakes made when first learning a new skill tend to be repeated and will need to be relearned. *Learn it correctly the first time, and repeat success.*

Speed at this point is not as important as legato, or an even tone, or even dynamics. Avoid accenting your thumb during cross-overs or cross-unders. Each note should be smoothly connected to the next, without "false accents." Do not hold down a finger past the time the note is meant to be played. Do not hold down more than one note at a time.

When you're ready, set the metronome to 60–72 bpm, and practice eighth notes for two octaves, and then four octaves. Practice at faster tempos or sixteenth notes as you become familiar with the notes and fingerings.

It is helpful to practice the scales in groups where the fingerings are the same. Major scales in the key of C, D, E, G, and A all have the same fingerings, and practicing them together will really drill the standard 123 1234 5 (left hand: 5 4321 321) pattern.

IMPROVISATION CORNER

The major scale is used to improvise and create melodies in all genres. Some examples of tunes that use the major scale in the melody are "As Time Goes By" by Herman Hupfeld (first sixteen measures), "There Will Never Be Another You" by Harry Warren, "St. Thomas" by Sonny Rollins, and "Higher Power" by Coldplay (chorus).

Set up a Latin drum beat, and vamp on a B♭6 chord with your left hand. Run the B♭ major scale up and down to get it in your ear. *Drill the correct fingering!* Then improvise your own melodies. Make up your own rhythms, and enjoy the rhythmic feel!

"Tommy" is an etude featuring the B♭ major scale in the melody. Play the chords in your left hand as written, and analyze the use of the B♭ major scale in the melody. Put on your favorite Latin drum beat, and play!

1. The first time, play the melody in both hands.
2. The second time, add the left-hand chords.

Tommy

FIG. 1.4. Major Scale Etude "Tommy"

LISTENING: MAJOR SCALE

"Ode to Joy," by Ludwig Van Beethoven, Liszt's transcription, performed by Igor Levit

"Somewhere Over the Rainbow," composed by Harold Arlen and Yip Harburg, performed by Ariana Grande

"Imagine," composed and performed by John Lennon

The Major Pentatonic and Minor Pentatonic Scales

The *major pentatonic scale* is a series of whole steps and minor thirds which form a five-note linear formation.

The interval structure for major pentatonic is: W W m3 W m3.

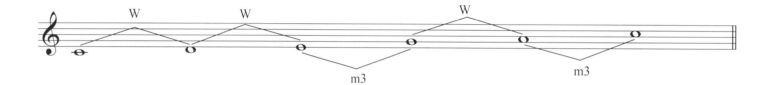

FIG. 2.1. C Major Pentatonic Scale Interval Structure

The major pentatonic scale's numbering is 1 2 3 5 6. Built on stacking a series of five perfect fifths (counting the root), it is missing the two half-steps found in the major scale. This makes for a scale without the need to resolve scale degrees 4 and 7 found in the major scale.

The *minor pentatonic scale* is the *relative minor* of the major pentatonic scale— that is, the same scale beginning on scale degree 6.

The interval structure for minor pentatonic is: m3 W W m3 W.

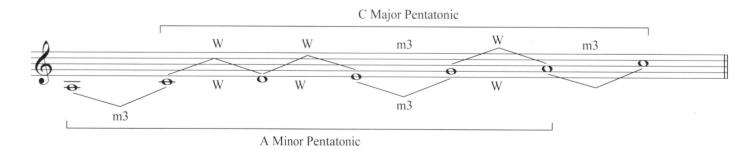

FIG. 2.2. A Minor Pentatonic vs. C Major Pentatonic Interval Structures (Relative Minor Relationship)

The minor pentatonic scale's degree numbering is 1 ♭3 4 5 ♭7. Again, these numbers relate to the parallel major scale's degrees. For example, the comparison of the C major scale and C minor pentatonic scale is:

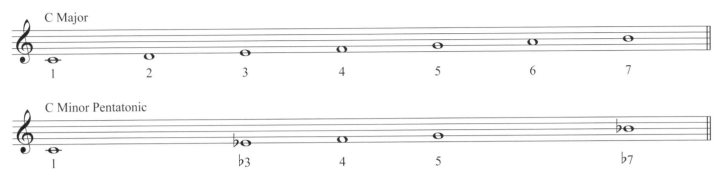

FIG. 2.3. Major Scale vs. Minor Pentatonic Scale

Pentatonic scales are widely used in pop, rock, jazz, folk, classical, and R&B music. Some examples are "Swing Low Sweet Chariot" by Wallace Willis, and "The Girl with the Flaxen Hair" by Claude Debussy.

TWELVE KEY STUDY

Practice the major pentatonic scale and its relative minor pentatonic scale together, one after the other. The notes and the fingerings are the same; just start on the root of either scale. The fingerings for both scales are written together: the first note starts with the root of the minor pentatonic scale, and the second note is the root of the major pentatonic scale. A good way to begin is with C major, F major, and G major pentatonic, as the fingerings are the same. Then work with A minor, D minor, and E minor pentatonic. This method will train your ear to the major and minor sounds.

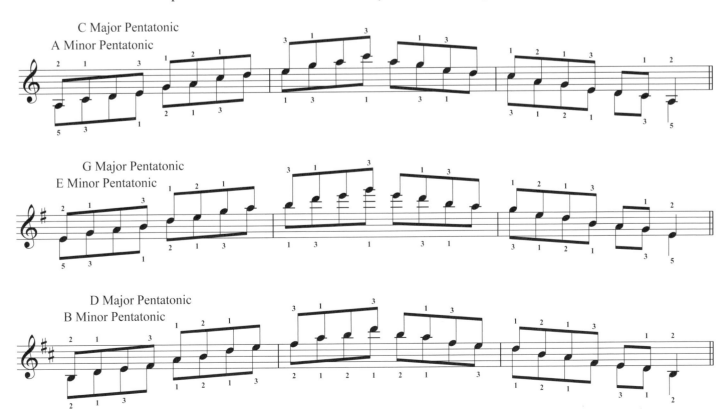

FIG. 2.4. Major and Minor Pentatonic Scales with Fingerings in Twelve Keys

IMPROVISATION CORNER

Play a major chord with your left hand, and run the major pentatonic scale improvising short phrases that you hear. Do the same with a minor seventh chord and the minor pentatonic scale. Create a vamp, and experiment!

"Amen" is a spiritual piece featuring the major pentatonic scale. It sounds best played as a solo piano piece.

Amen

FIG. 2.5. Major Pentatonic Etude "Amen"

"Lil' Lizard" is a tune that uses the minor pentatonic scale in the melody. It works great with a funk drum beat and the suggested bass line. Do you know what famous tune it's based on?

Lil' Lizard

FIG. 2.6. Minor Pentatonic Etude "Lil' Lizard"

LISTENING:

MAJOR PENTATONIC SCALE

"Amazing Grace," by John Newton and E.O. Excell, performed by Mahalia Jackson

"My Girl," composed by Smokey Robinson and Ronnie White, performed by the Temptations

MINOR PENTATONIC SCALE

"Chameleon," composed by Herbie Hancock, Paul Jackson, Bennie Maupin, and Harvey Mason, performed by Herbie Hancock

"Sonnymoon for Two," composed and performed by Sonny Rollins

CHAPTER 3

The Blues Scale

The blues scale is a series of minor thirds, whole steps, and half steps that form a six-note linear formation.

The interval structure is: m3 W ½ ½ m3 W.

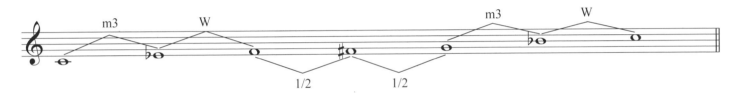

FIG. 3.1. C Blues Scale Interval Structure

The blues scale numbering is 1 ♭3 4 ♯4 5 ♭7. As usual, these numbers are in relationship to the parallel major scale. For example, the numbering of the C blues scale compared to the C major scale is:

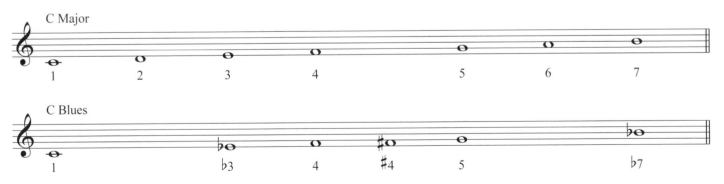

FIG. 3.2. Major Scale vs. Blues Scale

The blues scale can also be played starting on its second note, the ♭3. It gives the bluesy sound of a major pentatonic with a chromatic approach to its third degree.

FIG. 3.3. Blues Scale Beginning on ♭3

The blues scale can be heard in jazz, blues, and R&B/soul tunes. Blues lines are most often played descending the keyboard. Some pop tunes also have vocal riffs expressing "blue notes," such as the ♭3 and ♯4.

The blues scale is used over dominant seventh chords or any chord made to imply dominant or a bluesy sound.

TWELVE KEY STUDY

Practice the blues scale up and down the keyboard with both hands. Begin with two octaves. Then play the scale with your right hand, descending for four octaves while playing a syncopated dominant 7 chord in the left hand.

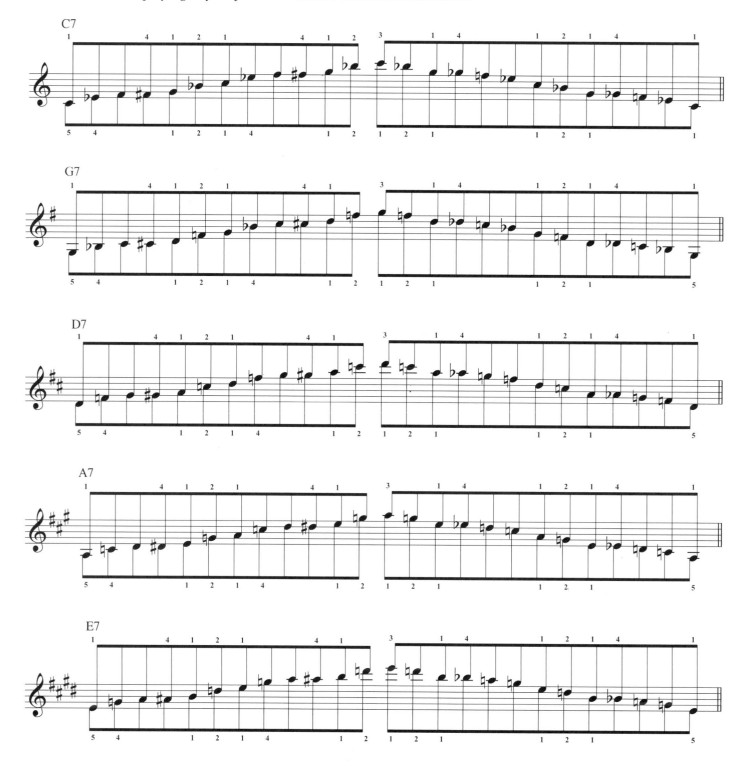

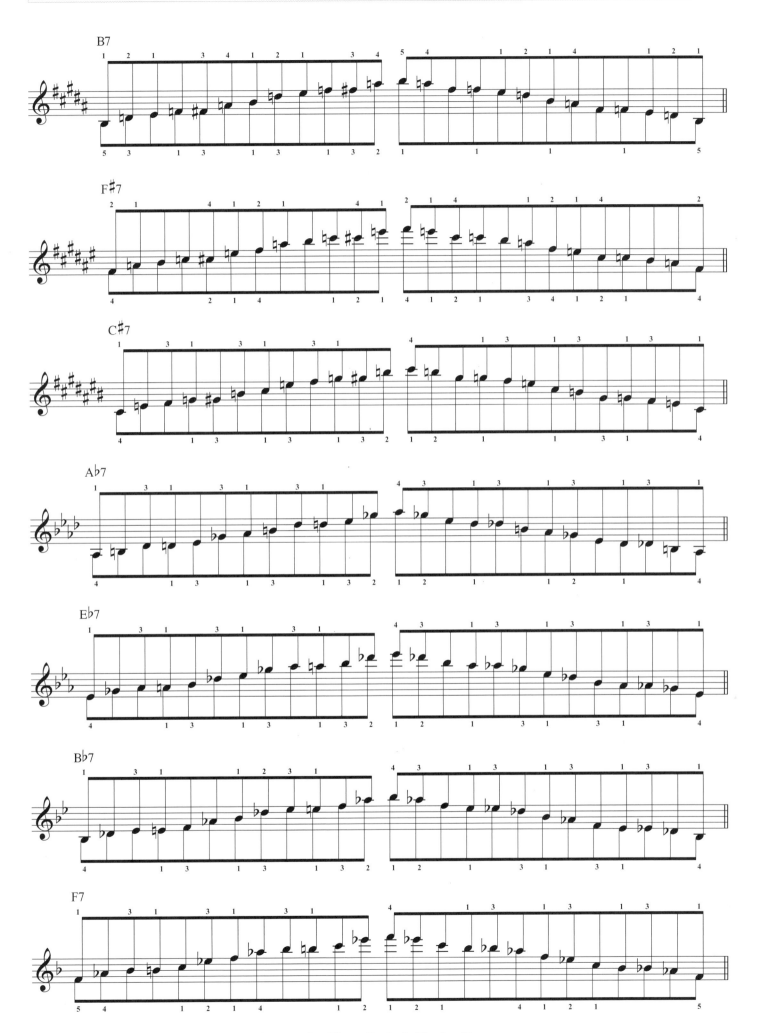

FIG. 3.4. Notes and Fingerings to the Blues Scale in Twelve Keys

IMPROVISATION CORNER

Put on your favorite drum beat, and play an F7 chord with your left hand. Run the F blues scale with you right hand, then play the phrases you hear. When you get the feel of it, expand to a twelve-bar blues, playing the left-hand chords throughout.

"Don't Muffle the Shuffle" is a bluesy tune showcasing the blues scale. Put on a shuffle drum beat, and play the melody and left-hand chords with the written rhythms.

Don't Muffle the Shuffle

FIG. 3.5. Blues Scale Etude "Don't Muffle the Shuffle"

LISTENING: THE BLUES SCALE

"The Thrill Is Gone," composed by Roy Hawkins and Rick Darnell, and performed by B.B. King

"Must Have Been the Devil," composed and performed by Otis Spann

"Blues for Alice," composed and performed by Charlie Parker

"Tenor Madness," composed and performed by Sonny Rollins

CHAPTER 4

Major Scale Modes

The modes of the major scale are the most widely studied and used modes. In order to find the modes (of any scale type), pick a *parent scale*—that is, the specific scale from which you can derive the modes by basing the mode's tonic on the different degrees of the parent scale. In this case, we will pick the C major scale as the parent scale. The characteristic chord for each mode is shown with stems and a beam.

To practice the different modes, play a seven-note group beginning on each degree of the parent scale. Each new tonic creates a mode with a different sound. The Greek names of the modes, structure, and numbering are indicated below.

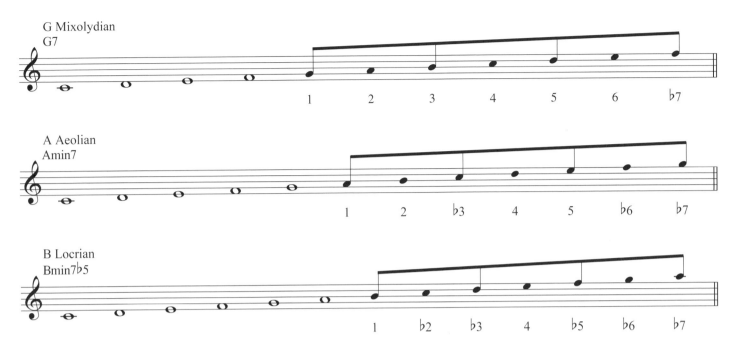

FIG. 4.1. Modes of C Major

The scale degree numbering of each mode is based on the comparison to its parallel major scale. For example, D Dorian compared to D major has two flats: ♭3 and ♭7 (F and C, vs. F♯ and C♯ in major).

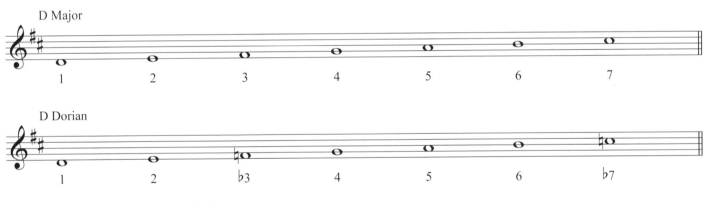

FIG. 4.2. Major vs. Dorian

Memorizing the scale degree numbering of each mode will teach you all of the modes in any key. For example, the spelling of G Lydian (♯4) and B♭ Mixolydian (♭7) is:

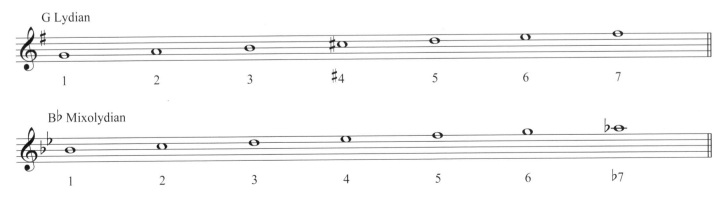

FIG. 4.3. G Lydian and B♭ Mixolydian Scale Degrees

While we may initially discover the modes by their relation to parent scales, do not only think of a mode as a major scale starting on a different note. Think of each modal sound in its own right. There is a big difference between the C major scale starting on D and the Dorian mode. The minor mode of Dorian is worlds away from a major tonality. D *must* be heard as the tonic of D Dorian; F *must* be heard as the ♭3. This is vastly different from a major scale starting on the second degree. The sound is most important! Center your ear on the tonic of each mode, and learn to admire the differences between them.

All diatonic scales and modes spell seventh chords. In order to find a scale's or mode's seventh chord, write out every other note of the mode starting on its root. For example, every other note of the C major scale is C E G B, which is a major seventh chord. Every other note of the D Dorian mode is D F A C, which is a minor seventh chord. The following table shows the type of seventh chord that correlates with each mode of the major scale.

	Major 7	Dominant 7	Minor 7	Minor 7♭5
Ionian	X			
Dorian			X	
Phrygian			X	
Lydian	X			
Mixolydian		X		
Aeolian			X	
Locrian				X

Modes of the major scale are widely used in jazz and other improvised art forms. Some well-known modal tunes are "All Blues" (Mixolydian/blues) and "Nardis" (Phrygian) by Miles Davis.

TWELVE KEY STUDY

While the goal is to be able to play all modes in twelve keys, a good place to start is Dorian and Mixolydian, as they correspond to the minor 7 and dominant 7 chords. Combined with the major scale, all the modes for a IImin7 V7 IMaj7 progression are studied.

The scales in figure 4.4 are written with fingerings for one octave; however, playing the scales for four octaves is the goal. In order to play four octaves, repeat the same fingering patterns written in the first octave. You may choose one key and play all six modes (parallel modes), or one mode in all twelve keys (relative modes).

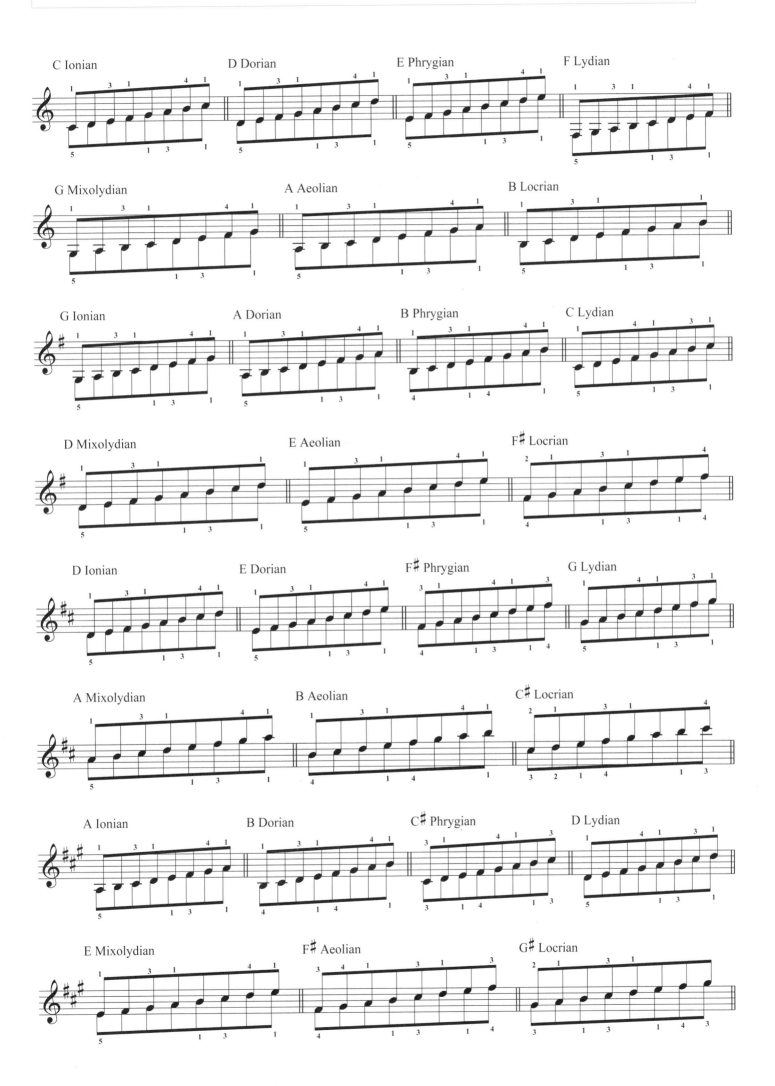

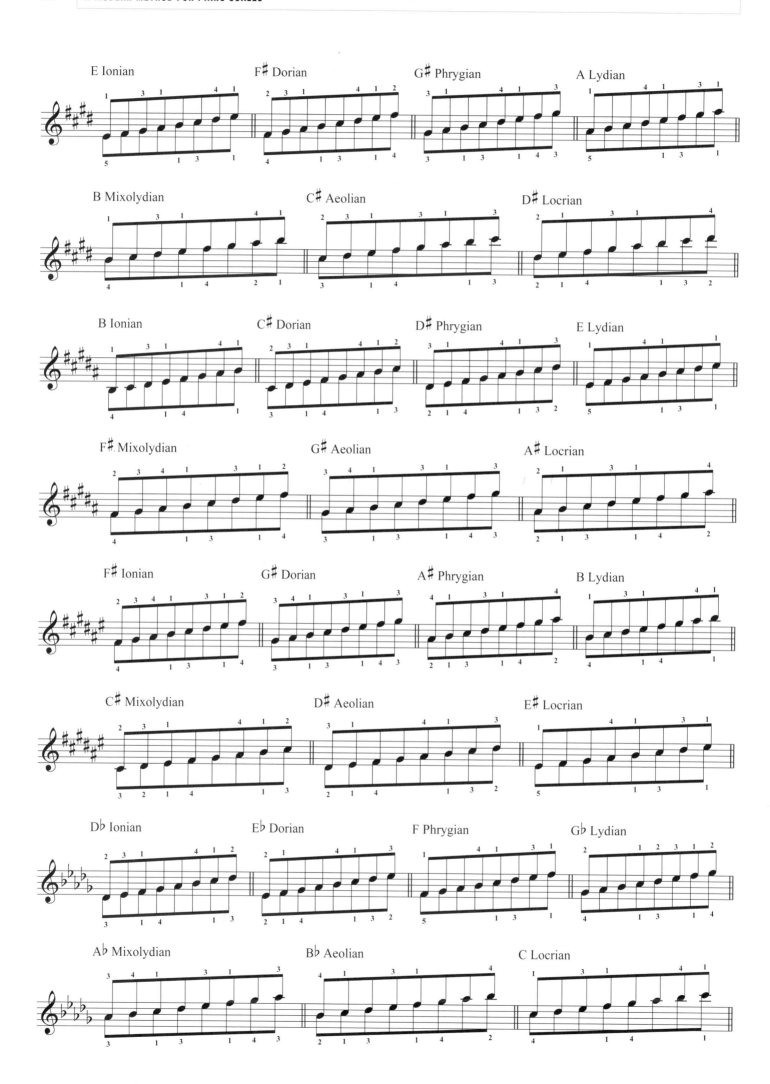

FIG. 4.4. Modes of Major Notes and Fingerings in Twelve Keys

IMPROVISATION CORNER

Choose a key and a mode, and create a two-chord modal vamp. Play seventh chords in your left hand, and improvise melodies in your right hand. Listen to the gentle movement between chords in this modal setting.

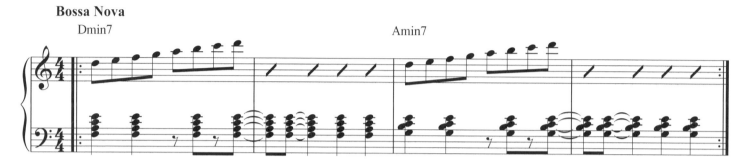

FIG. 4.5. D Dorian Modal Vamp

"Samba Yes!" is a Latin tune that uses the notes of the D Dorian mode in the melody. The Abdim7 is not from the Dorian mode, but adds some tension and release. Put on a beat, and play!

Samba Yes!

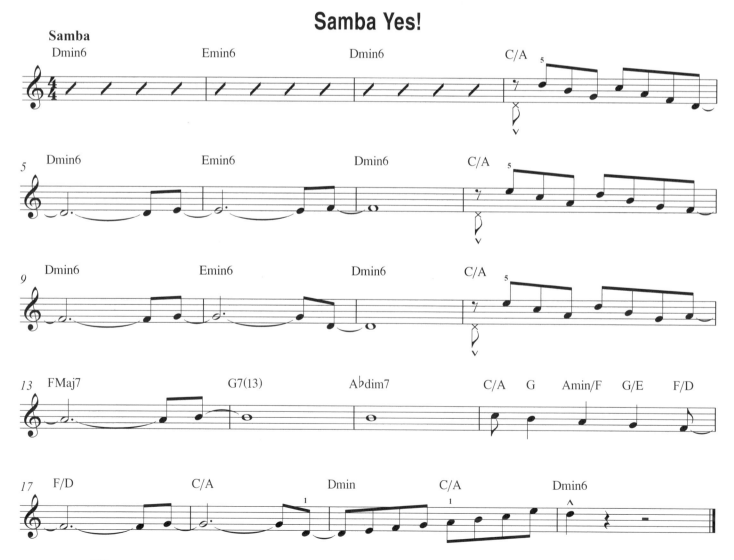

FIG. 4.6. Dorian Etude "Samba Yes!"

LISTENING:

DORIAN MODE

"Sorrow's End," composed and performed by Suzanna Sifter

"So What," composed and performed by Miles Davis

LYDIAN MODE

"Freewill," composed and performed by Rush

MIXOLYDIAN MODE

"Born This Way" composed and performed by Lady Gaga

CHAPTER 5

Jazz Melodic Minor Scale and Modes

The jazz melodic minor scale (and its modes) is one of the most extensively used scales in jazz. Jazz melodic minor is structured the same ascending and descending. This parent scale provides a great array of modes different from the modes of the major scale. The interval structure is: W ½ W W W W ½.

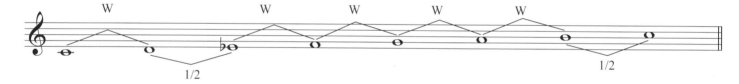

FIG. 5.1. C Jazz Melodic Minor Scale Interval Structure

To find its modes, begin on each scale degree. Some of the Greek modal names are the same as the major scale with some added accidentals.

In figure 5.2, the names of the modes, structure, scale-degree numbering, and seventh chords are labeled.

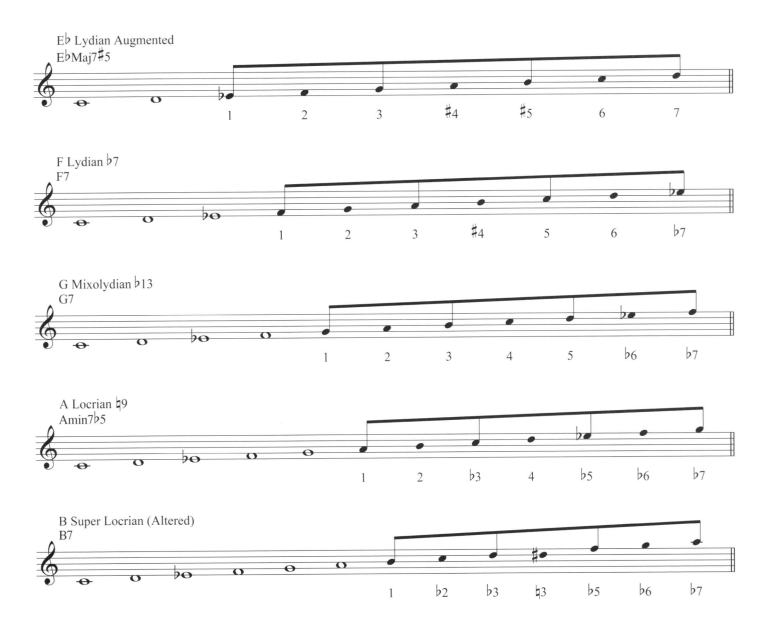

FIG. 5.2. Modes of Jazz Melodic Minor

Memorizing the scale degree numbering of each mode will teach you all of the modes in any key. For example, the numbering of F Lydian ♭7 and C altered are:

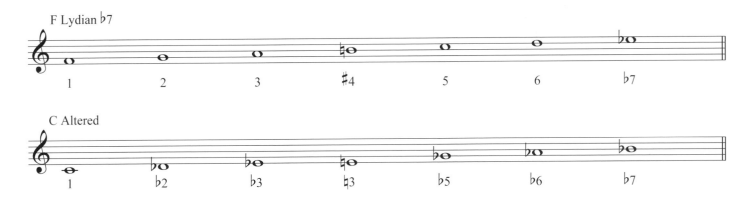

FIG. 5.3. F Lydian ♭7 and C Altered Scale Degrees

TWELVE KEY STUDY

The jazz melodic minor scale can be used to improvise in minor-key jazz tunes such as "Blue Bossa" by Kenny Dorham and "Summertime" by George Gershwin. Different modes have vastly different sounds and functions. Learn to hear each mode with its corresponding seventh chord:

	Augmented Major 7	Dominant 7	Minor 7	Minor Major 7	Minor 7♭5
Jazz Melodic Minor				X	
Dorian ♭9			X		
Lydian Augmented	X				
Lydian ♭7		X			
Mixolydian ♭13		X			
Locrian ♮9					X
Altered		X			

Through repetition, twelve key study really opens the ear to the sounds of these modes. Play the corresponding seventh chords in your left hand as you improvise modal lines with your right hand.

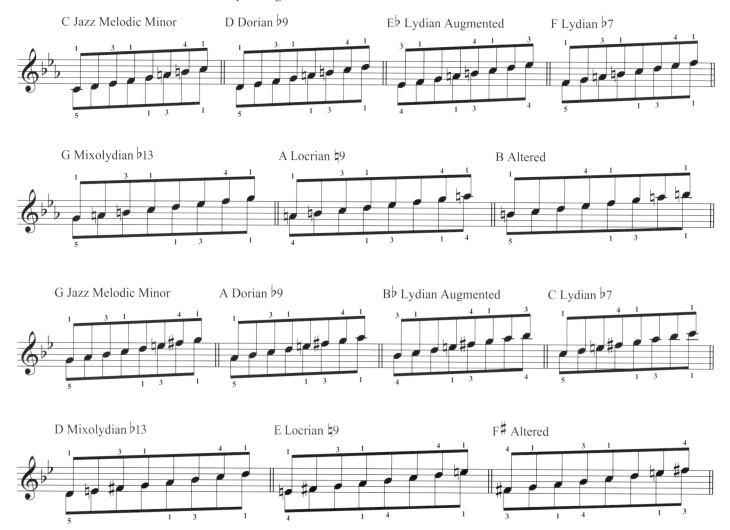

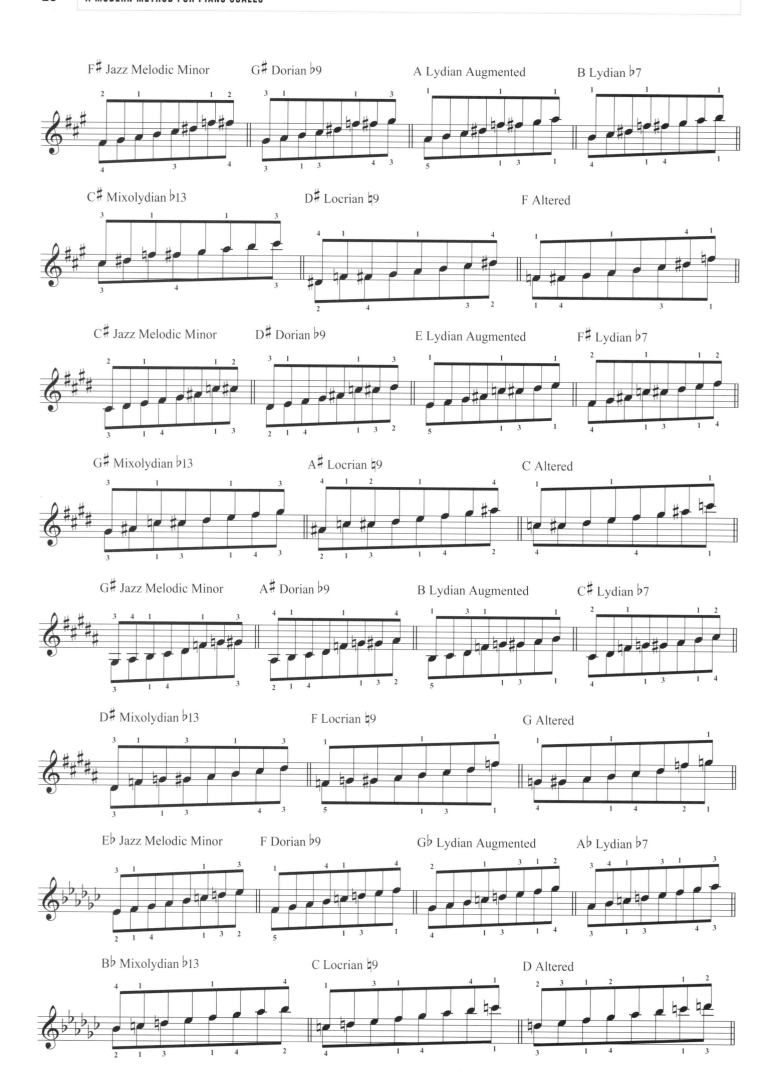

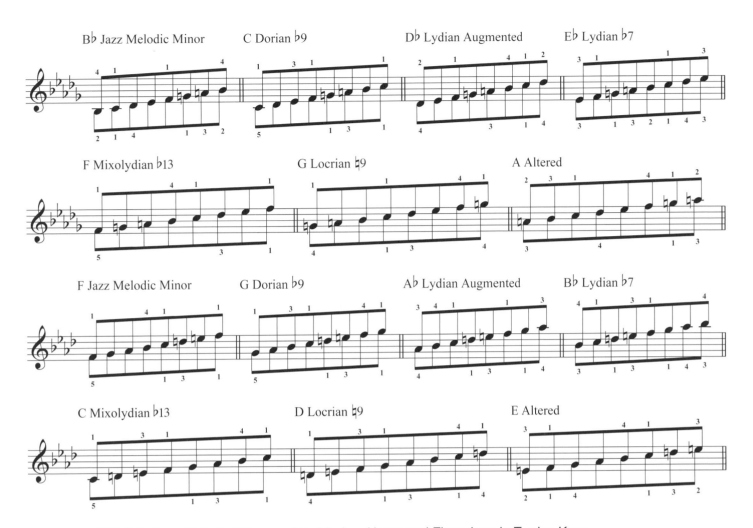

FIG. 5.4. Jazz Melodic Minor and Its Modes, Notes and Fingerings in Twelve Keys

IMPROVISATION CORNER

The sound of the jazz melodic minor scale combines the natural 6 and 7 with the ♭3—a minor sonority with a major sonority. This creates colorful differences in the modes, such as Lydian Augmented and Lydian ♭7. Each mode has its own diatonic seventh chord, as shown in figure 5.2. Choose a key and two modes to create a two- to three-chord vamp. Play the seventh chords in your left hand and improvise melodies you hear in your right hand. Creating a musical context in which to practice the modes is a significantly more enjoyable way to practice!

FIG. 5.5. Lydian ♭7 and Altered Vamp

"A Simple Melody" is a slow and gentle New Age piece. Play both hands as written. Analyze the scale degrees in the melody.

A Simple Melody

FIG. 5.6. Jazz Melodic Minor Scale Etude "A Simple Melody"

LISTENING: MELODIC MINOR SCALE

"Lush Life" (bridge), composed by Billy Strayhorn, performed by Esperanza Spalding

"Windows" (first twelve bars), composed and performed by Chick Corea

CHAPTER 6

Harmonic Major and Harmonic Minor Scales and Modes

The harmonic major and harmonic minor scales and modes are widely used in jazz and Latin jazz. The ♭6 and major 7 in the scale creates the characteristic augmented second sound of these scales. It also creates a V7 chord with a ♭9 or ♭9/♭13. These parent scales create a substantial selection of modes different from the modes of the major or jazz melodic minor scales, the difference being a ♭6 combined with either a natural or ♭3. The interval structures are:

- Harmonic Major: W W ½ W ½ m3 ½
- Harmonic Minor: W ½ W W ½ m3 ½

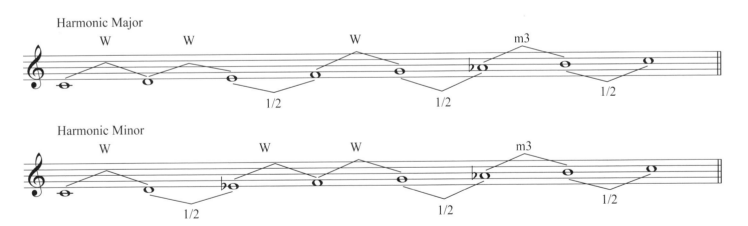

FIG. 6.1. C Harmonic Major vs. C Harmonic Minor Interval Structures

In order to find the modes, begin on each scale degree of each parent scale. Some of the Greek modal names are the same as the major scale but in a different order and written with additional accidentals. The seventh chords of each mode are identified. The names of the modes, structure, and scale degree numbering are indicated.

Here are the modes of harmonic major:

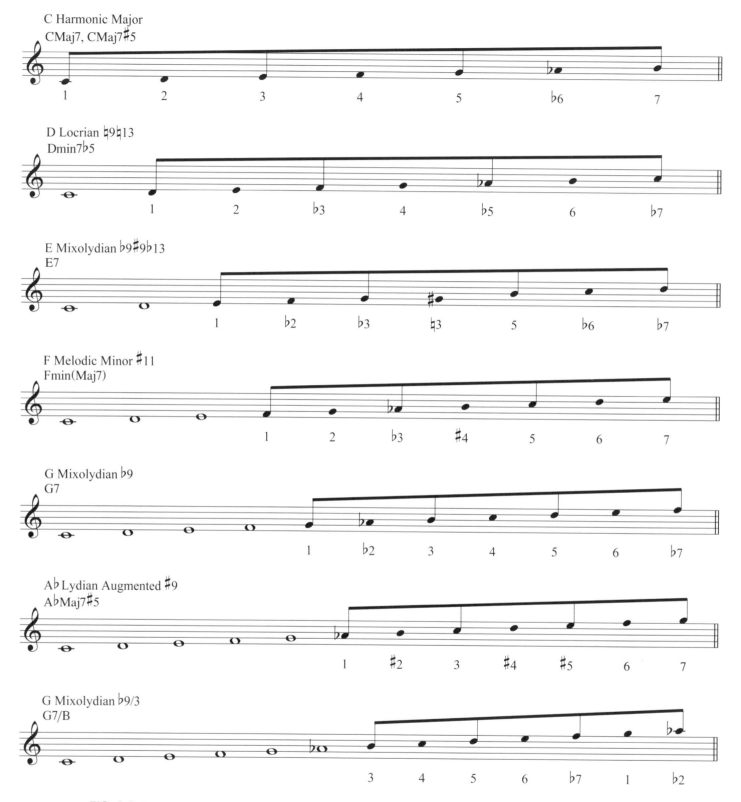

FIG. 6.2. Modes of Harmonic Major

Here are the modes of harmonic minor.

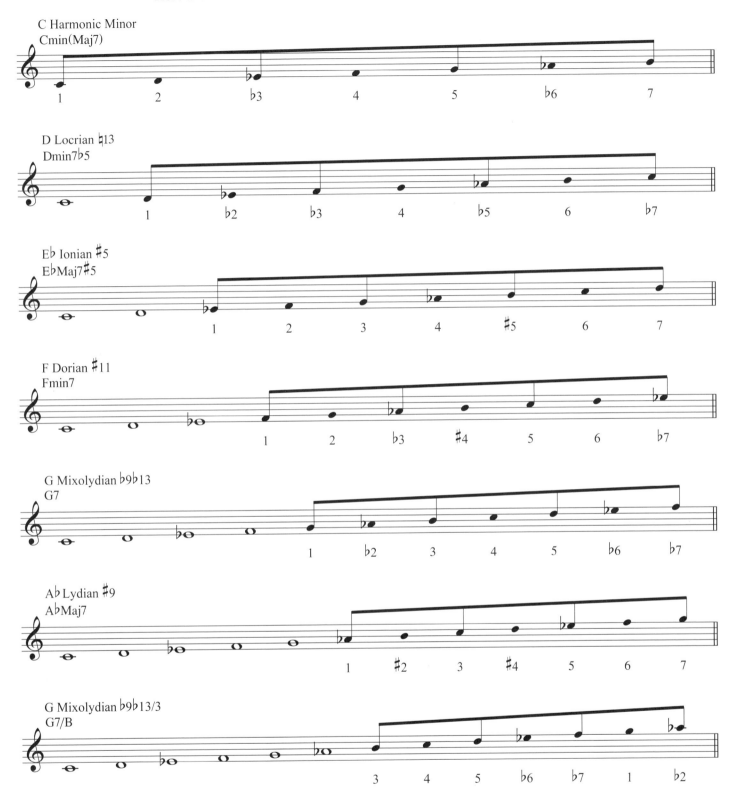

FIG. 6.3. Modes of Harmonic Minor

Memorizing the scale degree numbering of each mode will quickly teach you any of the modes in any key. For example, the spellings of the fifth modes, G Mixolydian ♭9 and G Mixolydian ♭9 ♭13, are:

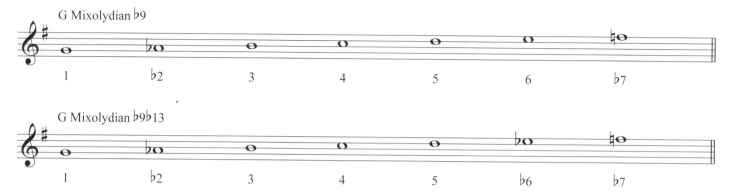

FIG. 6.4. G Mixolydian ♭9 and G Mixolydian ♭9 ♭13 Scale Degrees

TWELVE KEY STUDY

An effective way to practice the parent scales is to play both scales (e.g., harmonic major and harmonic minor) in one key. In this way, you can compare the fingerings and sound of the scales. Next, practice the modes in two to four keys at a time. Remember that while ultimately the goal is to know all modes in twelve keys, set attainable goals for success.

Harmonic Major

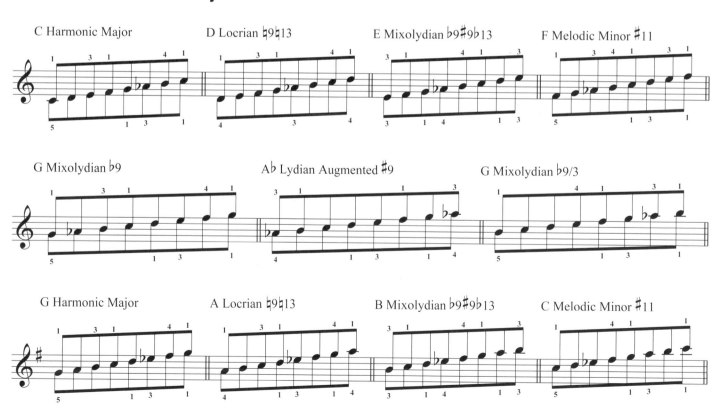

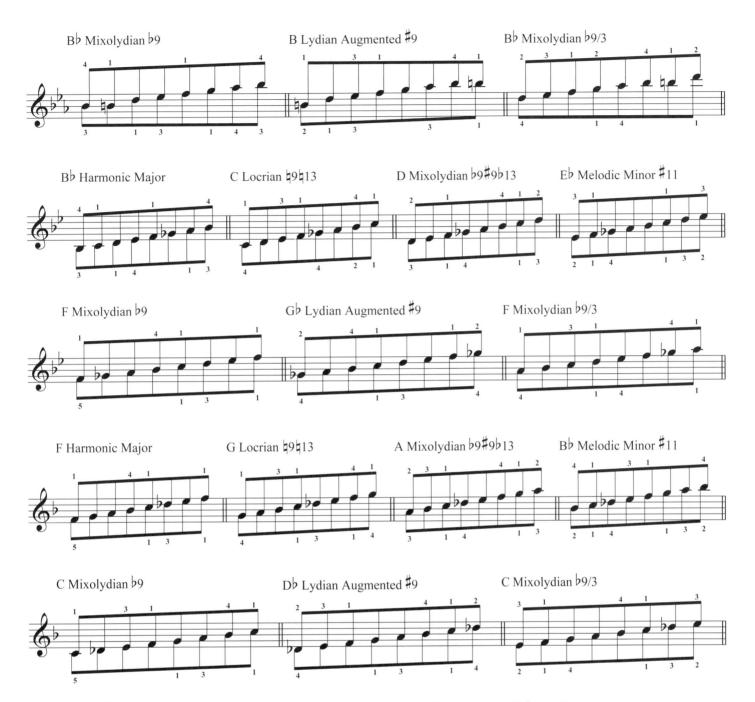

FIG. 6.5. Harmonic Major Scale and Modes, Notes and Fingerings in Twelve Keys

Harmonic Minor

Many styles of music incorporate the harmonic minor scale, but often switch between other forms of the minor scales. Examples are "What Are You Doing the Rest of Your Life" by Michelle LeGrand and "Girl" by the Beatles.

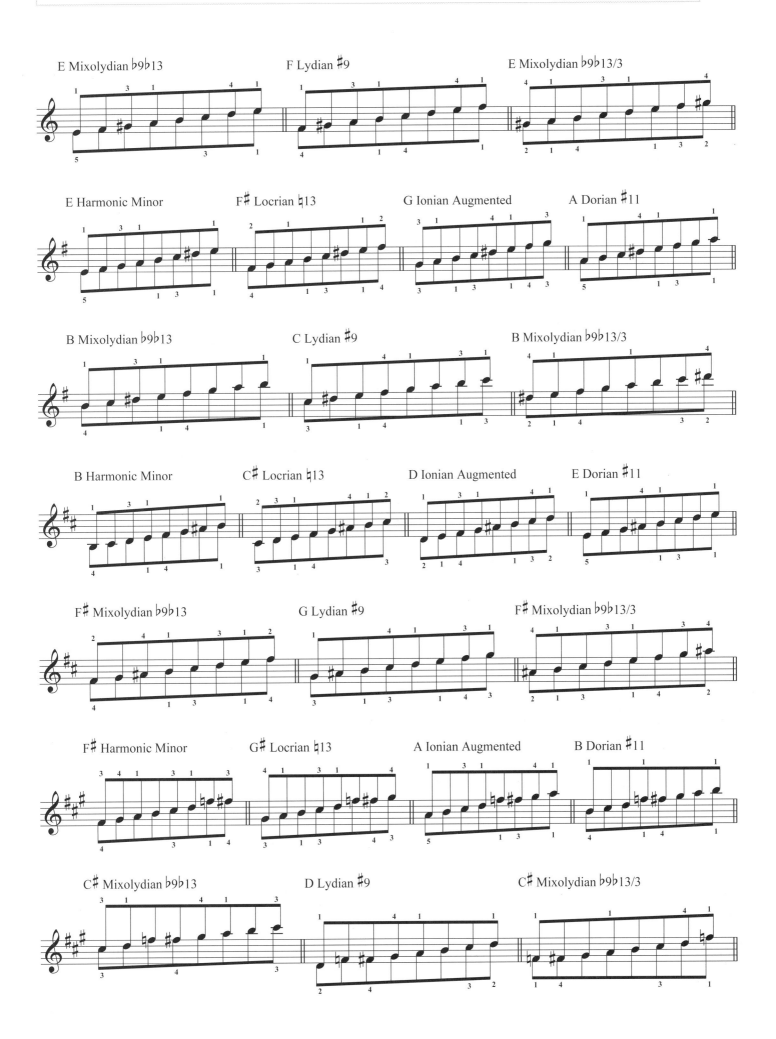

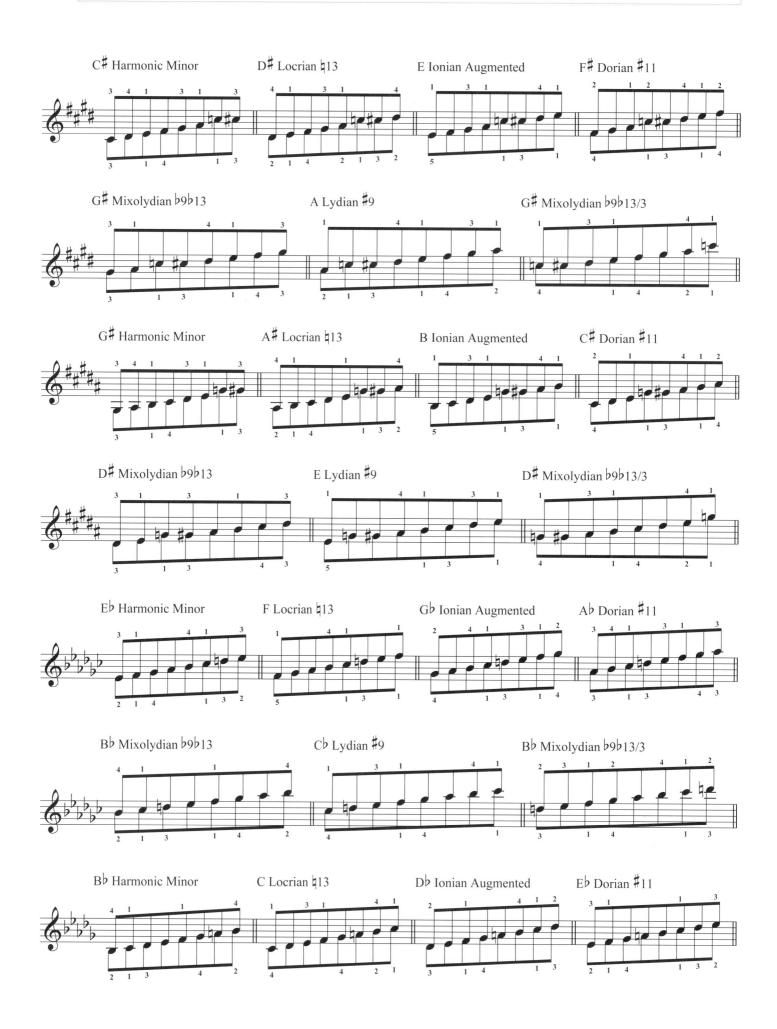

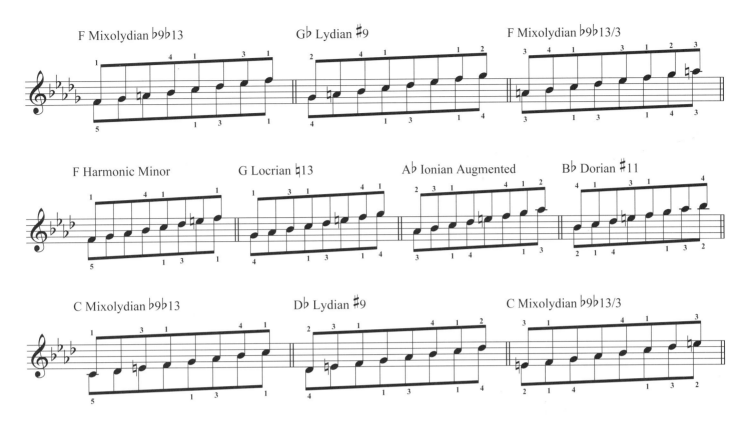

FIG. 6.6. Harmonic Minor Scale and Its Modes, Notes and Fingerings in Twelve Keys

IMPROVISATION CORNER

The combination of either the major or minor 3 with the ♭6 and natural 7 creates the major-minor sound in harmonic major and authentic minor sound in harmonic minor. The characteristic sound of these scales is the ♭6 coupled with the raised 7. You can feature these notes when improvising or composing. Each mode has its own diatonic 7 chord, as shown in the following charts.

Harmonic Major

	Major 7♯5	Minor Major 7	Dominant 7	Minor 7♭5
Harmonic Major	X			
Locrian ♮9/13				X
Mixolydian ♭9 ♯9 ♭13			X	
Melodic Minor ♯11		X		
Mixolydian ♭9			X	
Lydian Augmented ♯9	X			
Mixolydian ♭9/3			X	

Harmonic Minor

	Major 7	Major 7#5	Minor 7	Minor Major 7	Dominant 7	Minor 7♭5
Harmonic Minor				X		
Locrian ♮13						X
Ionian #5		X				
Dorian #11			X			
Mixolydian ♭9 ♭13					X	
Lydian #9	X					
Mixolydian ♭9 ♭13/3					X	

Choose a key, and practice a V7 Imin(Maj) (or IMaj7) cadence as written below. Create a melody and play the seventh chords in your left hand. Work with this progression in two or three other keys. Remember, it is imperative to follow technical studies in a creative context!

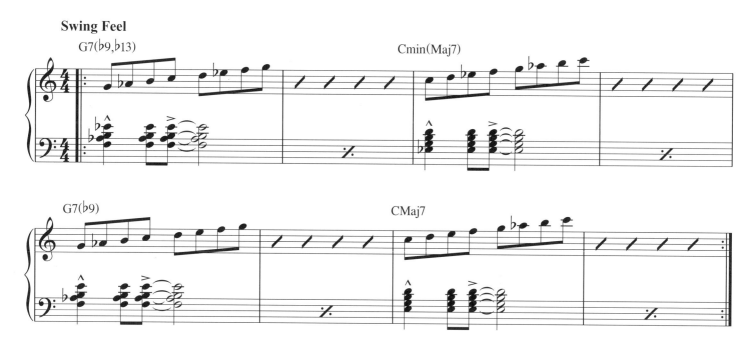

FIG. 6.7. V I Vamp

"Goodbye" is a pop ballad highlighting the harmonic major scale in the melody. Be sure to play it with both hands, and notice the IVmin and IImin7♭5 chords coloring the melody with diatonic harmonic major chords.

Goodbye

FIG. 6.8. Harmonic Major Etude "Goodbye"

"Blue Musaeus" is a lively bossa nova tune showcasing the harmonic minor scale. Notice how the augmented second between the ♭6 and major 7 is featured.

Blue Musaeus

FIG. 6.9. Harmonic Minor Etude "Blue Musaeus"

LISTENING: HARMONIC MINOR SCALE

"What Are You Doing the Rest of Your Life?," composed by Alan Bergman and Michel Legrand, performed by Barbra Streisand

"Invention No. 4," composed by J. S. Bach, performed by Glenn Gould

"Bury a Friend," composed by Billie Eilish and Finneas O'Connell, performed by Billie Eilish

"Sweet Dreams (Are Made of This)," composed by Annie Lennox and Dave Stewart, performed by the Eurythmics

CHAPTER 7

The Bebop Scales

"Bebop scales" were named as such because they were developed by jazz improvisers starting in the 1940s, the Bebop Era. There are three main forms of the bebop scale. The *major bebop scale* is based on the major scale, the *dominant bebop scale* is based on the Mixolydian mode, and the *altered bebop scale* is based on the Mixolydian ♭9 ♭13 mode. These scales are often played descending because the added half steps resolve down to the ♭7, 5, or root. The added chromatic notes create an eight-note scale.

The interval structures are as follow:

- Major bebop: ½ W ½ ½ W ½ W W
- Dominant bebop: ½ ½ ½ W W ½ W W
- Altered bebop: ½ ½ W ½ W ½ m3 ½

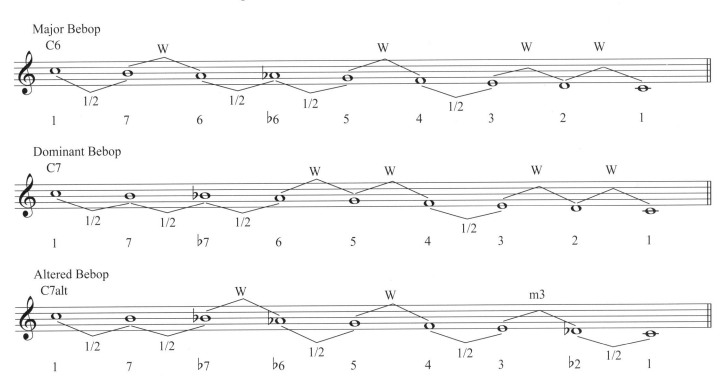

FIG. 7.1. C Major Bebop, Dominant Bebop, and Altered Bebop Scales Interval Structures

Bebop scales really evoke the chromatic sound of the players of the bebop era, such as Thelonious Monk, Bud Powell, Dizzy Gillespie, and Charlie Parker. Some bebop tunes are "A Night in Tunisia" by Dizzy Gillespie, "Donna Lee" by Charlie Parker and Miles Davis, and "Celia" by Bud Powell. You will find much usage of these scales in the improvisation of the musicians in these tunes.

TWELVE KEY STUDY

Practice the bebop scales with their respective seventh chords. For example, begin with a CMaj6 chord in your left hand, and play the C major bebop scale for two octaves descending in your right hand. Next play a dom7 chord and the dominant bebop scale the same way. Finish with a dom7(♭9,♭13) in your left hand, and play the altered bebop scale in your right hand. Continue through the circle of fifths.

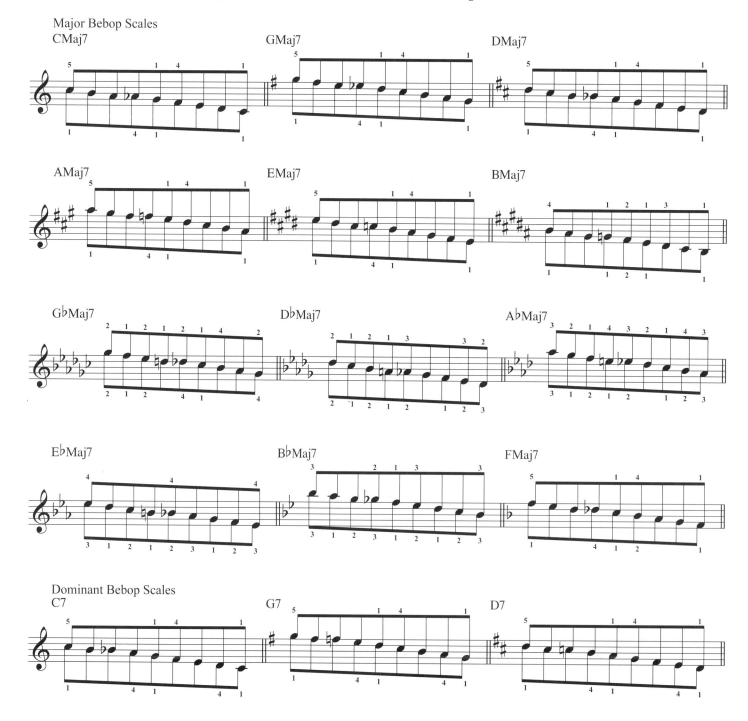

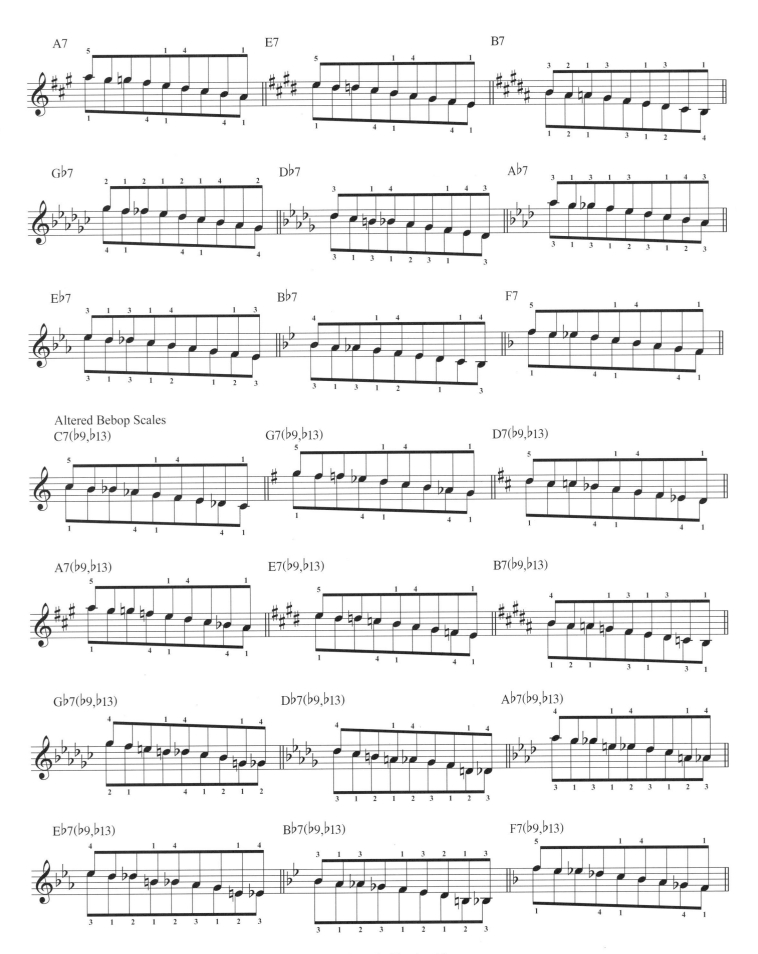

FIG. 7.2. Bebop Scales Notes and Fingerings in Twelve Keys

IMPROVISATION CORNER

A V7 IMaj6 progression is a good place to start with the bebop scale. You can start the major bebop scale on scale degrees 1, 6, 5, or 3, and both of the dominant bebop scales on scale degrees 1, ♭7, 5, or 3. Mix up the sounds, and play what you hear!

The following is an example of this V7 IMaj6 progression. Practice until you can play it with ease, then transpose to different keys.

FIG. 7.3. V I Chord Progression Using Bebop Scales

"Boppin'" is a jazz tune that features all three bebop scales discussed in this chapter. Notice how the half steps add tension and release. Play this tune with a swing feel.

Boppin'

FIG. 7.4. Bebop Scale Etude "Boppin'"

LISTENING: BEBOP SCALE

"Donna Lee" (melody and improvisation), composed and performed by Charlie Parker

"Confirmation" (improvisation), composed and performed by Charlie Parker

"Hallucinations," composed and performed by Bud Powell

CHAPTER 8

The Chromatic and Whole Tone Scales

The chromatic and whole tone scales are *symmetrical*; each is made up of an interval that repeats. The chromatic scale is all half steps, and the whole tone scale is all whole steps. The chromatic scale contains all twelve notes within an octave; the whole tone scale contains six notes.

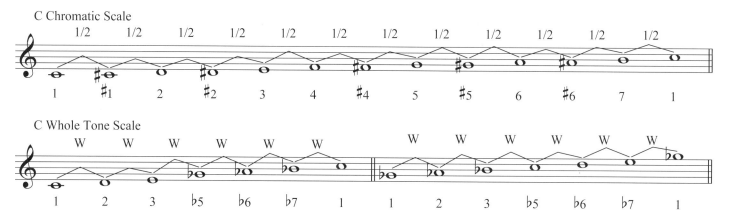

FIG. 8.1. Chromatic vs. Whole Tone Scales Interval Structures

While the chromatic scale doesn't correspond to a particular chord type, the whole tone scale corresponds to a dom7#5 chord. The chromatic and whole tone scales are used a lot in jazz, Latin jazz, and classical music. Often found in scalar runs, each creates a particular sound that craves a resolution. For example, the V7#5 chord with a whole tone melody wants to resolve to its IMaj7 chord.

FIG. 8.2. Dom7#5 Chord Using the Whole Tone Scale Resolving to IMaj7

TWELVE KEY STUDY

The chromatic scale can be played starting on any note, with the same fingering throughout because there is only one fingering. This makes twelve key practice simple. The whole tone scale has two fingerings: one beginning on C, and the other on D♭. Practice the whole tone scale starting on C, and then play through D, E, G♭, A♭, and B♭. Then play D♭, E♭, F, G, A, and B.

FIG. 8.3. Chromatic and Whole Tone Scales Notes and Fingerings

Listen to Thelonious Monk's "Straight, No Chaser" or Nikolai Rimsky-Korsakov's "Flight of the Bumblebee" to hear the chromatic scale in motion. The whole tone scale can be heard in Emerson, Lake & Palmer's "The Three Fates."

IMPROVISATION CORNER

Adding chromaticism in a jazz solo works well. You don't have to use the entire scale; even three or four notes create the desired effect.

The whole tone sound is more recognizable and is saved for augmented dominant occasions. (Note that the dom7♯5 partners with a ♮9.) Try running some lines using each scale over a dom7♯5.

FIG. 8.4. G7♯5 and C7♯5 Vamp

"N.A." is a jazz blues in the key of F. The chromatic scale targets various chord tones. The melody has a tricky "over the bar line" rhythm to the melody, so be sure to count!

N.A.

FIG. 8.5. Chromatic Scale Etude "N.A."

"Whole Tone Blues" has a 12/8 Afro-Cuban beat, with a melody in an eighth-note triplet feel. Notice how the whole tone scales target the chord tones.

Whole Tone Blues

FIG. 8.6. Whole Tone Scale Etude "Whole Tone Blues"

LISTENING:

CHROMATIC SCALE

"Straight, No Chaser," composed and performed by Thelonious Monk

"Blue Monk," composed and performed by Thelonious Monk

WHOLE TONE SCALE

"Voiles," *Preludes Book 1* No. 2, by Claude Debussy, performed by Anna Tsybuleva

"You Are the Sunshine of My Life" (Introduction), composed and performed by Stevie Wonder

CHAPTER 9

Symmetric Dominant, Diminished, and Augmented Scales

The symmetric dominant and diminished scales (abbreviated as *sym dom* and *sym dim*) are eight-note scales built with two repeating intervals:

- Sym Dom: ½ W
- Sym Dim: W ½

These scales are also called "combination diminished" because the sym dom is built with two diminished chords a half step apart, and the sym dim is built with two diminished chords a whole step apart.

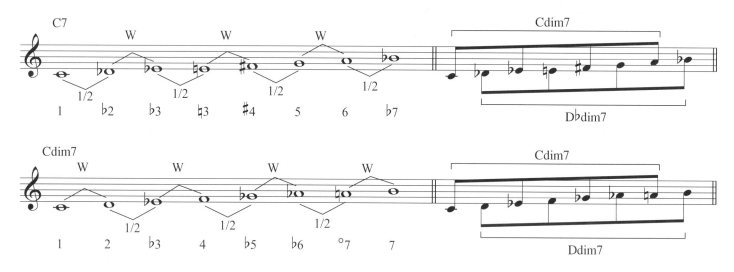

FIG. 9.1. Sym Dom vs. Sym Dim Scales and Combination Diminished Interval Structures

While both scales are sometimes called "sym dim," this text considers the half step/whole step scale "sym dom." This is because the scale also spells a dom7 chord, with tensions ♭9, ♯9, ♯11, and 13.

FIG. 9.2. Symmetric Dominant Scale and Dominant 7 Chord

The symmetric augmented scale (abbreviated as "sym aug") contains six notes with the repeating intervals of a minor third and half step. This scale is structured with two augmented triads a minor third apart.

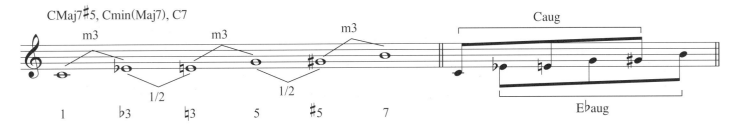

FIG. 9.3. Sym Aug Scale and Augmented Chord Interval Structures

Often used in scalar runs, the symmetric scales work especially well in sequential patterns. There are a few "avoid notes" in the sym aug scale, which may be looking for resolution (or not!). The sym aug scale contains a ♯9 and ♭13, and also a major 7; however, the major 7 can sound like a chromatic approach when resolved to the tonic.

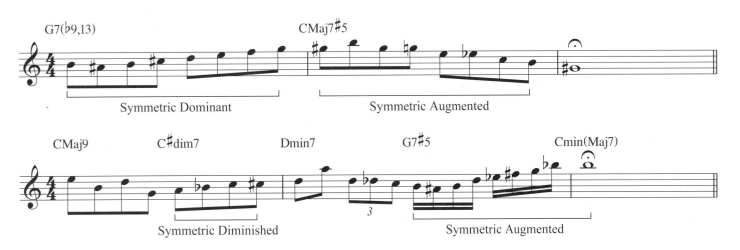

FIG. 9.4. Use of Symmetric Scales in Common Progressions

These symmetric scales are widely used in jazz, classical, and film music. Listen to Herbie Hancock's solo on "Freedom Jazz Dance" (by Miles Davis, on *Miles Smiles*). The sym aug is particularly noted for use in modern jazz improvisation. Listen to John Coltrane's "One Up, One Down."

TWELVE KEY STUDY

The fingerings for sym dom/dim/aug mainly use fingers 1, 2, and 3. The symmetrical nature of the symmetric dominant/diminished scales creates three scales, as there are three different diminished seventh chords until the first one repeats. There are four symmetric augmented scales, as there are four augmented triads until the first one repeats in inversion. The fingerings to the symmetric dominant/diminished scales are written starting on three different notes, and the symmetric augmented is written starting on four different notes.

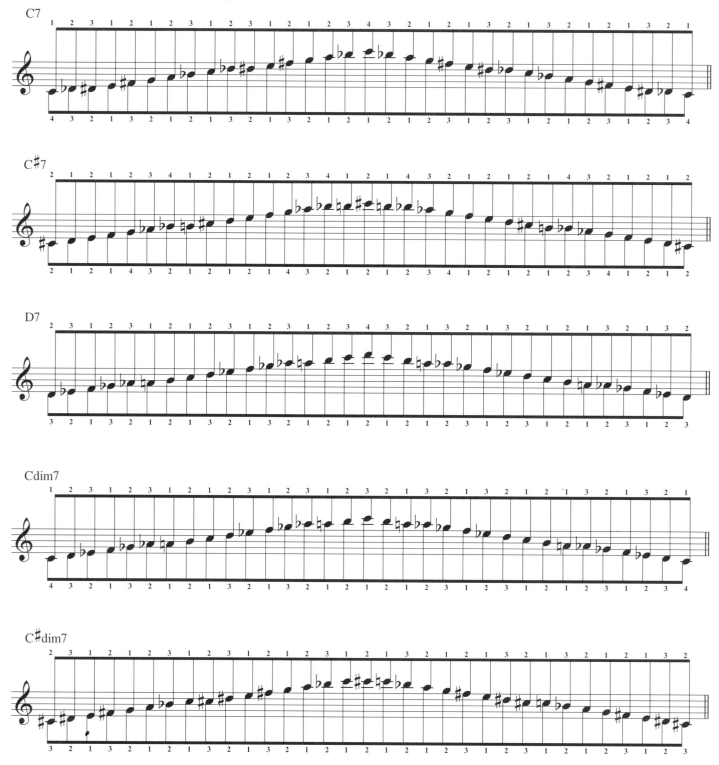

Ddim7

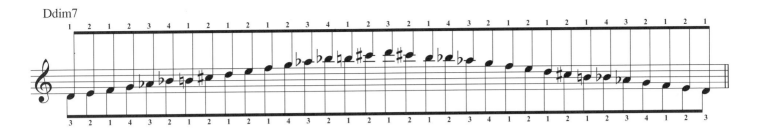

FIG. 9.5. Symmetric Dominant/Diminished Scales Notes and Fingerings

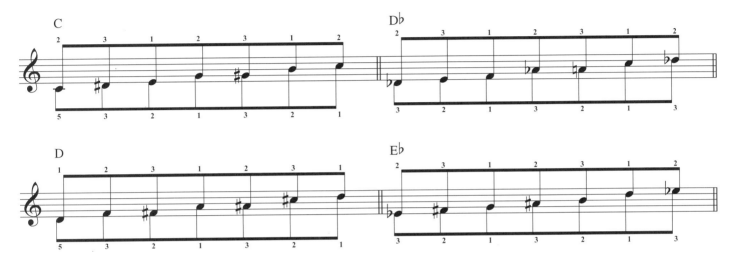

FIG. 9.6. Symmetric Augmented Scales Notes and Fingerings

IMPROVISATION CORNER

The symmetrical intervals in these scales each have a particular sound and drive. As in the chromatic and whole tone scales, you don't have to use the entire scale; even six notes create the desired effect. Try running some lines using each scale over their corresponding seventh chords.

FIG. 9.7. Vamps Based on Symmetric Dominant, Diminished, and Augmented Scales

"Op. 1" is a modern jazz tune featuring the sym dom, sym dim, and sym aug scales.
Notice how the striking sounds of the melody color the harmony.

Op. 1

FIG. 9.8. Symmetric Dominant, Diminished, and Augmented Scales Etude "Op. 1"

LISTENING: SYMMETRIC SCALES

"Freedom Jazz Dance" (piano solo), composed by Eddie Harris, performed by Herbie Hancock (on *Miles Smiles*)

"Opus Pocus," performed and composed by Jaco Pastorius

"Straphangin'," performed and composed by the Brecker Brothers

CONCLUSION

The study of music—be it of scales, chords, pieces, or improvisation—is a great joy. Don't forget to follow all your technical studies with a spirited musical piece. Good luck in your search for the perfect sounds you crave to hear!

—Suzanna M. Sifter

ABOUT THE AUTHOR

Photo by Portriat Simple

Suzanna M. Sifter is a jazz pianist and educator who has been on faculty in the piano department at Berklee College of Music since 1989. She holds a bachelor of music from Berklee and a master's in jazz performance from New England Conservatory.

Ms. Sifter has four recordings as a leader, composer/arranger, and pianist: *Flowers for You*, *Awakening*, *The Illumination*, and *Sophisticated Lady*. She is author of *Berklee Jazz Keyboard Harmony; Using Upper-Structure Triads*, which includes a unique collection of jazz piano performances.

Ms. Sifter has performed with John La Porta and Alan Dawson, and has recorded with Tony Lada, Larry Monroe, Greg Badolato, John Lockwood, Yoron Israel, Casey Scheuerell, Bruce Gertz, and Dino Govoni. Her compositions have been featured on *In the Library* (Dino Govoni) and *On the Edge* (Tony Lada).

Passionate about her teaching, Ms. Sifter has traveled extensively with Berklee to places such as Europe, South America, the U.S., Canada, and Japan giving master classes and performing. Over the years, she has taught her organized and inventive methods to thousands of successful students.

More Fine Publications

Berklee Press

GUITAR

BLUES GUITAR TECHNIQUE
by Michael Williams
50449623 Book/Online Audio $27.99

BERKLEE GUITAR CHORD DICTIONARY
by Rick Peckham
50449546 Jazz – Book $14.99
50449596 Rock – Book............................$12.99

BERKLEE GUITAR STYLE STUDIES
by Jim Kelly
00200377 Book/Online Media............$24.99

CLASSICAL TECHNIQUE FOR THE MODERN GUITARIST
by Kim Perlak
00148781 Book/Online Audio...............$19.99

CONTEMPORARY JAZZ GUITAR SOLOS
by Michael Kaplan
00143596 Book..$16.99

COUNTRY GUITAR STYLES
by Mike Ihde
00254157 Book/Online Audio..............$24.99

CREATIVE CHORDAL HARMONY FOR GUITAR
by Mick Goodrick and Tim Miller
50449613 Book/Online Audio.............$22.99

FUNK/R&B GUITAR
by Thaddeus Hogarth
50449569 Book/Online Audio.............$19.99

GUITAR SWEEP PICKING
by Joe Stump
00151223 Book/Online Audio................$19.99

JAZZ GUITAR FRETBOARD NAVIGATION
by Mark White
00154107 Book/Online Audio..............$22.99

JAZZ GUITAR IMPROVISATION STRATEGIES
by Steven Kirby
00274977 Book/Online Audio.............$24.99

JAZZ SWING GUITAR
by Jon Wheatley
00139935 Book/Online Audio..............$24.99

MODAL VOICINGS FOR GUITAR
by Rick Peckham
00151227 Book/Online Media..............$24.99

A MODERN METHOD FOR GUITAR*
by William Leavitt
Volume 1: Beginner
00137387 Book/Online Video..............$24.99
Other volumes, media options, and supporting songbooks available.

A MODERN METHOD FOR GUITAR SCALES
by Larry Baione
00199318 Book...$14.99

TRIADS FOR THE IMPROVISING GUITARIST
by Jane Miller
00284857 Book/Online Audio............$22.99

BASS

BASS LINES
Fingerstyle Funk
by Joe Santerre
50449542 Book/Online Audio $19.99
Metal
by David Marvuglio
00122465 Book/Online Audio $19.99
Rock
by Joe Santerre
50449478 Book/Online Audio $22.99

BERKLEE JAZZ BASS
by Rich Appleman, Whit Browne, and Bruce Gertz
50449636 Book/Online Audio $22.99

FUNK BASS FILLS
by Anthony Vitti
50449608 Book/Online Audio............ $22.99

INSTANT BASS
by Danny Morris
50449502 Book/CD $9.99

READING CONTEMPORARY ELECTRIC BASS
by Rich Appleman
50449770 Book.. $22.99

VOICE

BELTING
by Jeannie Gagné
00124984 Book/Online Media $22.99

THE CONTEMPORARY SINGER
by Anne Peckham
50449595 Book/Online Audio $27.99

JAZZ VOCAL IMPROVISATION
by Mili Bermejo
00159290 Book/Online Audio $19.99

TIPS FOR SINGERS
by Carolyn Wilkins
50449557 Book/CD...................................... $19.95

VOCAL WORKOUTS FOR THE CONTEMPORARY SINGER
by Anne Peckham
50448044 Book/Online Audio..........$24.99

YOUR SINGING VOICE
by Jeannie Gagné
50449619 Book/Online Audio $29.99

WOODWINDS/BRASS

TRUMPET SOUND EFFECTS
by Craig Pederson and Ueli Dörig
00121626 Book/Online Audio...............$14.99

TECHNIQUE OF THE SAXOPHONE
by Joseph Viola
50449820 Volume 1....................................$19.99
50449830 Volume 2....................................$22.99
50449840 Volume 3....................................$22.99

PIANO/KEYBOARD

BERKLEE JAZZ KEYBOARD HARMONY
by Suzanna Sifter
00138874 Book/Online Audio............ $29.99

BERKLEE JAZZ PIANO
by Ray Santisi
50448047 Book/Online Audio $22.99

BERKLEE JAZZ STANDARDS FOR SOLO PIANO
Arranged by Robert Christopherson, Hey Rim Jeon, Ross Ramsay, Tim Ray
00160482 Book/Online Audio.............. $19.99

CHORD-SCALE IMPROVISATION FOR KEYBOARD
by Ross Ramsay
50449597 Book/CD...................................$19.99

CONTEMPORARY PIANO TECHNIQUE
by Stephany Tiernan
50449545 Book/DVD $29.99

HAMMOND ORGAN COMPLETE
by Dave Limina
00237801 Book/Online Audio $24.99

JAZZ PIANO COMPING
by Suzanne Davis
50449614 Book/Online Audio $22.99

LATIN JAZZ PIANO IMPROVISATION
by Rebecca Cline
50449649 Book/Online Audio............ $29.99

SOLO JAZZ PIANO
by Neil Olmstead
50449641 Book/Online Audio.............$42.99

DRUMS/PERCUSSION

BEGINNING DJEMBE
by Michael Markus and Joe Galeota
00148210 Book/Online Video...............$16.99

BERKLEE JAZZ DRUMS
by Casey Scheuerell
50449612 Book/Online Audio.............$24.99

DRUM SET WARM-UPS
by Rod Morgenstein
50449465 Book...$14.99

DRUM STUDIES
by Dave Vose
50449617 Book...$12.99

A MANUAL FOR THE MODERN DRUMMER
by Alan Dawson and Don DeMichael
50449560 Book...$14.99

MASTERING THE ART OF BRUSHES
by Jon Hazilla
50449459 Book/Online Audio.............$19.99

PHRASING: ADVANCED RUDIMENTS FOR CREATIVE DRUMMING
by Russ Gold
00120209 Book/Online Media $19.99

WORLD JAZZ DRUMMING
by Mark Walker
50449568 Book/CD $22.99

Berklee Press publications feature material developed at the Berklee College of Music.
To browse the complete Berklee Press Catalog, go to **www.berkleepress.com**

STRINGS/ROOTS MUSIC

BERKLEE HARP
Chords, Styles, and Improvisation for Pedal and Lever Harp
by Felice Pomeranz
00144263 Book/Online Audio............$24.99

BEYOND BLUEGRASS
Beyond Bluegrass Banjo
by Dave Hollander and Matt Glaser
50449610 Book/CD $19.99

Beyond Bluegrass Mandolin
by John McGann and Matt Glaser
50449609 Book/CD $19.99

Bluegrass Fiddle and Beyond
by Matt Glaser
50449602 Book/CD $19.99

CONTEMPORARY CELLO ETUDES
by Mike Block
00159292 Book/Online Audio............$19.99

EXPLORING CLASSICAL MANDOLIN
by August Watters
00125040 Book/Online Media..........$24.99

FIDDLE TUNES ON JAZZ CHANGES
by Matt Glaser
00120210 Book/Online Audio............$16.99

THE IRISH CELLO BOOK
by Liz Davis Maxfield
50449652 Book/Online Audio..........$27.99

JAZZ UKULELE
by Abe Lagrimas, Jr.
00121624 Book/Online Audio............$22.99

BERKLEE PRACTICE METHOD

GET YOUR BAND TOGETHER
With additional volumes for other instruments, plus a teacher's guide.
Bass
by Rich Appleman, John Repucci, and the Berklee Faculty
50449427 Book/CD $24.99

Drum Set
by Ron Savage, Casey Scheuerell, and the Berklee Faculty
50449429 Book/CD $17.99

Guitar
by Larry Baione and the Berklee Faculty
50449426 Book/CD $19.99

Keyboard
by Russell Hoffmann, Paul Schmeling, and the Berklee Faculty
50449428 Book/Online Audio $14.99

MUSIC BUSINESS

CROWDFUNDING FOR MUSICIANS
by Laser Malena-Webber
00285092 Book....................$17.99

HOW TO GET A JOB IN THE MUSIC INDUSTRY
by Keith Hatschek with Breanne Beseda
00130699 Book....................$27.99

MAKING MUSIC MAKE MONEY
by Eric Beall
00355740 Book....................$29.99

MUSIC LAW IN THE DIGITAL AGE
by Allen Bargfrede
00366048 Book $24.99

PROJECT MANAGEMENT FOR MUSICIANS
by Jonathan Feist
50449659 Book....................$34.99

THE SELF-PROMOTING MUSICIAN
by Peter Spellman
00119607 Book....................$24.99

MUSIC THEORY/EAR TRAINING/ IMPROVISATION

BEGINNING EAR TRAINING
by Gilson Schachnik
50449548 Book/Online Audio $17.99

THE BERKLEE BOOK OF JAZZ HARMONY
by Joe Mulholland and Tom Hojnacki
00113755 Book/Online Audio............$29.99

BERKLEE CORRESPONDENCE COURSE
00244533 Book/Online Media...........$29.99

BERKLEE EAR TRAINING DUETS AND TRIOS
by Gaye Tolan Hatfield
00284897 Book/Online Audio...........$19.99

BERKLEE MUSIC THEORY
by Paul Schmeling
50449615 **Rhythm, Scales Intervals** $24.99
50449616 **Harmony**.....................$24.99

CONDUCTING MUSIC TODAY
by Bruce Hangen
00237719 Book/Online Video............$24.99

IMPROVISATION FOR CLASSICAL MUSICIANS
by Eugene Friesen with Wendy M. Friesen
50449637 Book/CD $24.99

JAZZ DUETS
by Richard Lowell
00302151 C Instruments........................ $14.99

MUSIC NOTATION
by Mark McGrain
50449399 Theory and Technique....$24.99

REHARMONIZATION TECHNIQUES
by Randy Felts
50449496 Book...........................$29.99

MUSIC PRODUCTION & ENGINEERING

AUDIO MASTERING
by Jonathan Wyner
50449581 Book/CD...................$29.99

AUDIO POST PRODUCTION
by Mark Cross
50449627 Book...................$19.99

CREATING COMMERCIAL MUSIC
by Peter Bell
00278535 Book/Online Media...........$19.99

THE SINGER-SONGWRITER'S GUIDE TO RECORDING IN THE HOME STUDIO
by Shane Adams
00148211 Book/Online Audio..............$19.99

UNDERSTANDING AUDIO
by Daniel M. Thompson
00148197 Book...................$42.99

WELLNESS/AUTOBIOGRAPHY

LEARNING TO LISTEN: THE JAZZ JOURNEY OF GARY BURTON
00117798 Book...........................$34.99

MANAGE YOUR STRESS AND PAIN THROUGH MUSIC
by Dr. Suzanne B. Hanser and Dr. Susan E. Mandel
00117798 Book...........................$34.99

MUSICIAN'S YOGA
by Mia Olson
50449587 Book...........................$19.99

THE NEW MUSIC THERAPIST'S HANDBOOK
by Suzanne B. Hanser
00279325 Book...........................$29.99

SONGWRITING/COMPOSING/ ARRANGING

ARRANGING FOR HORNS
by Jerry Gates
00121625 Book/Online Audio..............$22.99

ARRANGING FOR STRINGS
by Mimi Rabson
00190207 Book/Online Audio...........$22.99

BEGINNING SONGWRITING
by Andrea Stolpe with Jan Stolpe
00138503 Book/Online Audio $22.99

BERKLEE CONTEMPORARY MUSIC NOTATION
by Jonathan Feist
00202547 Book...........................$24.99

COMPLETE GUIDE TO FILM SCORING
by Richard Davis
50449607 ....$34.99

CONTEMPORARY COUNTERPOINT
by Beth Denisch
00147050 Book/Online Audio...........$24.99

COUNTERPOINT IN JAZZ ARRANGING
by Bob Pilkington
00294301 Book/Online Audio...........$24.99

THE CRAFT OF SONGWRITING
by Scarlet Keys
00159283 Book/Online Audio...........$22.99

CREATIVE STRATEGIES IN FILM SCORING
by Ben Newhouse
00242911 Book/Online Media...........$27.99

ESSENTIAL SONGWRITING
by Jonathan Feist & Jimmy Kachulis
50448051 ....$10.99

JAZZ COMPOSITION
by Ted Pease
50448000 Book/Online Audio $39.99

MELODY IN SONGWRITING
by Jack Perricone
50449419 Book...........................$24.99

MODERN JAZZ VOICINGS
by Ted Pease and Ken Pullig
50449485 Book/Online Audio...........$24.99

MUSIC COMPOSITION FOR FILM AND TELEVISION
by Lalo Schifrin
50449604 Book...........................$39.99

MUSIC NOTATION
50449540 **Preparing Scores & Parts**.....$24.99
50449399 **Theory and Technique**...........$24.99

POPULAR LYRIC WRITING
by Andrea Stolpe
50449553 Book...........................$16.99

SONGWRITING: ESSENTIAL GUIDE
by Pat Pattison
50481582 **Lyric and Form Structure** $19.99
00124366 **Rhyming** $22.99

SONGWRITING IN PRACTICE
by Mark Simos
00244545 Book...........................$16.99

SONGWRITING STRATEGIES
by Mark Simos
50449621 Book...........................$24.99

THE SONGWRITER'S WORKSHOP
by Jimmy Kachulis
50449519 **Harmony** $29.99
50449518 **Melody** $24.99

Prices subject to change without notice. Visit your local music dealer or bookstore, or go to **halleonard.com** to order